INSULT

The Ultimate Shortcut Handbook to Winning Every Argument

Jax Joust

Lazy Cotton Publishing

PREFACE

For too long, we've been told to turn the other cheek when dealing with rude people. We've been taught that kindness and understanding are the best ways to diffuse difficult situations. But what about those people who are so unpleasant, so rude, that they seem to delight in making our lives miserable? Is it really fair to let them get away with their bad behavior?

I've spent my whole life trying to be kind to these people, to show them that there's a better way to live. But I've come to realize that sometimes, the best way to deal with rude people is to give them a taste of their own medicine. Sometimes, it's not worth the energy to be kind back to those who don't deserve it.

That's why I've put together this book of insults for dealing with rude people. From the intellectually challenged to the downright unpleasant, these people deserve their own medicine. It's time to stop wasting our energy trying to be kind to those who don't deserve it, and start standing up for ourselves.

Of course, this book is not a license to be rude to everyone. We should still treat normal people with kindness and respect. But for those who make our lives miserable, who delight in being unpleasant, it's time to fight fire with fire. Let them work on themselves and their behavior, and let us take care of ourselves.

With great power comes great responsibility.

Jax Joust

CONTENTS

Intelligence: For those moments when you're stuck with someone who's as bright as a broken light bulb, these insults will help you avoid being dragged into their abyss of ignorance and save yourself from a headache. Especially those who try to patronize and belittle you. Give them a dose of medicine.

"Your intellect resembles a black hole, infinitely dense yet devoid of any light."

"If ignorance were a sport,

you'd be a world champion."

"Your thoughts are like radio static: irritating and impossible to decipher."

"Your ideas hold as much water as a sieve."

"You're the proof that

evolution can go in reverse.

Charisma and social skills: When you're stuck with someone who's about as charming as a wet blanket at a party, these insults will help you gracefully excuse yourself from their company and move on to someone more engaging. These are great burns to kick those rude people off of their high horses.

"You have the charisma of a wet sock at a dinner party."

"You possess the charm of a mosquito at a blood drive."

"Your personality is akin to the Bermuda Triangle, where good vibes mysteriously vanish."

"Your social skills are like a faulty GPS, constantly leading you astray."

"Your presence is as enjoyable as an unsolicited robocall."

Humor and wit: For those compulsive banterers who think they're hilarious but couldn't crack a smile on a cadaver, these insults will help you laugh in their face and move on to someone more amusing. I've specially crafted these for those who use "joking" as an excuse to be rude to you. Break their glass shield with these bullets dipped in salt.

"Your wit is much like a desert mirage: seemingly promising, yet ultimately nonexistent."

"Your sense of humor is as dry as the Sahara Desert."

"You're like a broken record,
but with less nostalgic charm."

"Your attempts at humor are as successful as a lead balloon."

Uselessness and unhelpfulness: When someone's contribution is about as useful as a chocolate teapot in a kitchen fire, these insults will help you point out their lack of productivity and avoid being dragged down by their incompetence. When they aren't trying to help and they're either trying to be passive aggressive or just going through the motions of existing in your work unit or even "support group" by punching the clock with their counterfeit help.

"Your conversation skills are like a broken pencil: utterly pointless and in desperate need of sharpening."

"Your words hold as much weight as a helium balloon."

"You're about as useful as a chocolate teapot in a forest fire."

"Your ideas are as groundbreaking as a cracked sidewalk."

"Your input is as valuable as counterfeit money.

Unpleasantness and annoyance: For those moments when someone's presence is about as enjoyable as a root canal without anesthesia, these insults will help you tell them to hit the road and avoid being driven insane by their unbearable behaviour.

"You're the human embodiment of a migraine."

"Your voice is like nails on a chalkboard, but less pleasant."

"You're as welcome as a snowstorm in the Sahara."

"Your company is as appealing as a root canal."

"You're like a mosquito at an orchestra, buzzing incessantly but contributing nothing."

Mediocrity and insignificance: When someone's about as interesting as a blank sheet of paper and their existence is about as relevant as a toothpick in a haystack, these insults will help you point out their lack of importance and move on to more meaningful interactions.

"You're the visual
representation of a dull ache."

"You're the walking
equivalent of an eye-roll."

"You're the reason the word 'unremarkable' exists."

"You're as inconsequential as a single grain of sand in the desert."

"You're as intriguing as an empty room."

Clumsiness and awkwardness: Use these insults to tell someone their skills are about as refined as a gorilla in a china shop and avoid being embarrassed by their lack of grace.

"You have the grace of a three-legged giraffe on ice skates."

"Your determination is like a squirrel crossing the road."

"You're like a human pop-up ad, always appearing at the worst moments."

"Your attention span is shorter than a goldfish with amnesia."

"You have the social aptitude of a garden gnome."

Unfulfilled potential and disappointment: For those who've never lived up to their potential and couldn't find success if it bit them in the backside, these insults will help you express your disappointment and avoid being dragged down by their mediocrity.

"You're the poster child for wasted potential."

"You're the epitome of wasted potential."

"You're the embodiment of a participation trophy."

"You're a perpetual underachiever in the school of life."

"You're the human embodiment of a disappointed sigh."

Negativity and unpleasantness: When someone's attitude is about as positive as a broken elevator and their presence is about as enjoyable as a colonoscopy, these insults will help you convey your annoyance and avoid being dragged down by their negativity.

"You're the reason aliens refuse to visit Earth."

"Your existence is the dictionary definition of mediocrity."

"You're the reason we can't have nice things."

"You're as enchanting as a wet blanket."

"You're like a parade on a rainy day: a damp, miserable spectacle."

Uselessness and unreliability: When someone's ideas and actions are about as reliable as a fortune cookie, these insults will help you tell them to get lost and avoid being disappointed by their incompetence.

"You're as reliable as a
sandcastle during high tide."

"Your train of thought has clearly derailed."

"You're as consistent as a chameleon in a room of mirrors."

"You're the human equivalent of a perpetual loading screen."

"You're as dependable as a melting ice sculpture."

Physical unattractiveness: When someone dares belittle your looks, use these insults to convey their own lack of physical appeal and avoid being insulted by their projections and repulsed by their unsightly features.

"Your face could launch a thousand ships... in the opposite direction."

"You have the allure of a trash fire."

"You have the charm of a cactus in a hug."

"You're as delightful as a stubbed toe."

"You're the human equivalent of elevator music."

Ineffectiveness and failure: When someone's track record is about as successful as a parachute that opens on impact, these insults will help you convey their lack of effectiveness and avoid being dragged down by their failure.

"You're as subtle as a sledgehammer in a glass factory."

"You have all the appeal of expired milk."

"You're the personification of wasted time."

"You have the staying power
of a house of cards in a hurricane."

"Your impact is like a whisper in a thunderstorm."

Annoyance and frustration: For those moments when someone's presence is about as tolerable as a toothache, these insults will help you tell them to hit the bricks and avoid being annoyed by their unbearable behaviour.

"Your presence is as enticing as a dental appointment."

"You're as helpful as a sundial at midnight."

"Your attention span is shorter than a goldfish with amnesia."

"You're the reason God created the middle finger."

"You're the personification of a dead-end street."

Lack of creativity or imagination: When someone's ideas are about as creative as a sack of potatoes, these insults will help you point out their lack of imagination and avoid being bored by their uninteresting thoughts.

"Your creativity is as barren as a lunar landscape."

"Your ideas are as groundbreaking as a cracked sidewalk."

"Your mind is as organized as a tornado in a thrift store."

"You have the presence of a wet firecracker."

"You're a master of mediocrity in a world of talent."

Incompetence or inadequacy: When someone's skills are about as adequate as a bicycle in a NASCAR race, these insults will help you convey their lack of competence and avoid being disappointed by their ineptitude.

"You're as captivating as a blank wall."

"Your attempts at humor are as successful as a lead balloon."

"Your impact is like a whisper in a thunderstorm."

"Your input is as valuable as counterfeit money."

"You're the personification of a hangnail."

Undesirability or repulsiveness: Use these insults to humorously convey someone's lack of appeal and avoid being repulsed by their unappealing features. These insults will help you tell them to beat it and avoid being stuck with their revolting presence.

"Your company is as appealing as a root canal."

"You're like an expired lottery ticket: full of false hope and disappointment."

"Your thoughts are as shallow as a puddle on a hot day."

"You have the magnetism of a slug in a salt mine."

"You're the reason the phrase 'bless their heart' was invented."

Failure to meet expectations: For those who never quite make the cut and couldn't achieve success if it was handed to them on a silver platter, these insults will help you express your disappointment and avoid being dragged down by their constant letdowns.

"You're like a puzzle with missing pieces: incomplete and frustrating."

"You're a monument to wasted opportunities."

"You're as dependable as a melting ice sculpture."

"You have the tenacity of a sloth on sedatives."

"Your attempts at humor are as successful as a lead balloon."

Overall unpleasantness: When someone's overall presence is about as welcome as a skunk in a perfume factory, these insults will help you tell them to take a hike and avoid being dragged down by their miserable demeanor. Use them to humorously convey your annoyance and to escape their unbearable company.

"Your existence is the
dictionary definition of mediocrity."

"Your presence is as uplifting as a lead balloon."

"You're the human equivalent of a dropped call."

"You're the poster child for unfulfilled dreams."

"Your impact is like a whisper in a thunderstorm."

EPILOGUE

And so it is, my dear reader, that we come to the end of this tome on the art of verbal sparring. As you close the book, I hope you feel a sense of empowerment, a feeling that you are now equipped with the necessary tools to hold your own in any battle of wits. But let me be clear, this is not a license to be cruel or abusive. No, this is about defending oneself, standing up for what you believe in, and making your voice heard.

In the world of ideas, there will always be those who seek to tear down, belittle, and silence. They will use every trick in the book to undermine your position, to make you doubt yourself, to make you feel small. But armed with a sharp tongue, a quick wit, and a healthy dose of self-confidence, you can meet them head-on, and emerge victorious.

Remember, however, that words can also be used for good. They can uplift, inspire, and bring people together. They can shine a light on injustice, expose hypocrisy, and give voice to the voiceless. So, while it is important to be able to hold your own in a battle of wits, it is equally important to use your words wisely, with compassion, and with the goal of making the world a better place.

In the words of one of the greats, "I have as much authority as the Pope, I just don't have as many people who believe it." So go forth, my dear reader, and use your newfound authority with care, with conviction, and with a touch of humor.

And with that, I bid you adieu, and may your words be forever sharp and your comebacks forever witty!

•

www.lazycotton.press

Printed in Great Britain
by Amazon

33515459R00066